Disconnected Memories

Disconnected Memories

poems by
Dominic Albanese

LEAKY BOOT PRESS

Disconnected Memories
by Dominic Albanese

First published in 2019 by
Leaky Boot Press
http://www.leakyboot.com

Copyright © 2019 Dominic Albanese
All rights reserved

No part of this book may be reproduced or transmitted in any form or by any means, electronic, mechanical, photocopying, recording, or otherwise, without prior written permission of the author.

ISBN: 978-1-909849-69-3

I must here thank—

Donna Lee Phillips
Corina Pelloni
Seb Doubinsky

and more other people than I can name, for their support and belief in me which has enabled me to believe in myself.

Contents

It Was	11
Dark Blue	12
The Saloon	14
Factors	15
There	16
A Bill Murray	18
The Wicked Queen	19
Naughty	20
The Way	21
Afternoon Rain	22
World's Oldest Woman	23
Space Rocks	24
Over the Moon	26
1966	27
52 Years Ago	28
TED Talk	30
C I B	31
Reach Back	32
Can Not Help Myself	34
Banjaxed	36
Lexonography	37
Love	38
Lozzem Game	39
Disturbed	40
Somewhere	41
A Bit	42
Ms Albright n Ms Feminismo	44
My Daughter	45
At Dinner	46

A Good Guy With a Gun	47
Impossible	48
Harmony	50
Made It	51
Forgiveness Sunday	52
Peck Slip	53
My Father	54
To Mourn	55
Mistaken Identity	56
Down Shift	57
Two	58
We Were	60
A Time	61
Eye Blink	62
Late	64
Fly Boy	65
Possible	66
Love Affairs	67
I Am	68
Sometimes	69
5:10 a.m.	70
Easy To	72
Clutter	73
Long Ago	74
Domestic Advice	75
No Bake Cookies	76
Silent Sorrows	78
Dust	79
Jan '64	80
Plants… Planets… People	82
Was More Than 40	83
Living History	84
Musta Been	86
Given a Gift	87
Azzuro Bene	88
Go Away	89
Sleepwalk	90
Ode to Dancing	92
Radio Love Song	93

Like the TV Show?	94
Air Water Salami Sandwich	95
Restore	96
Simplicity	97
Askance	98
Wondering	100
Brightly So	101
Tell Me	102
When	103
Umm Jumble Fly Getting By	104
Midway Blues	106
Me Too	107
Sisters	108
Mother's Day	110
I Would Be Remiss	112
Yesterday's Ring	113
Collected	114
41716	116
Last Week	117
Connective	118
A Love Poem	119
Was a Time	120
She	121
Unable	122
Some Times…	124
Neural Pathways	125
Holy Shitarolley	126
Two Rods	127
Been Shot	128
Another Week	130
Looking Back	131

It Was

Bob Kaufman
"when I die have no plans to stay dead"
age
of us all
now
artists… gangsters… wearing
either show garb
or
cloth of common man
pass
leave trails of recorded
written
painted
blood stained
memory
eternal

Dark Blue

not the music
kind
fleeting memories
glances
lace… smiles
places
past
torn romance

as if yesterday
was
really gone

that whole half empty glass
rigamarole… we move
we change… we grow or die

memories are part of a
price we all pay
to stay on the boat
afloat
O2 n chow… sleep… dreams… hopes… chances
life itself biggest chance
of all

now
as far away as "she" is
it does not matter
because she is not
a memory
she is a now

today… tomorrow
even dare
I say
from this day then
till there are no
more
tomorrows only that dark blue
memory… haunting
my
bones

The Saloon

keeper
had a mirror
installed
muted the ginrose nose
bloodshot eyes
dulled the bald spot glare
as
the silent stools lifted a glass
to One Leg Willy who
drank himself dead
the view
yes muted
the smell
of sad paychecks
sorrow lost love wishes hopes dreams
staggered to the urinal
one more for my baby
one more for the road
Frankie wails from a 1956 juke box
tears… cheers. who the fuck knows

Factors

as try to
match
morning stillness
mood
phase
moon phase
a sky without color
lush tropic branches
fruit tree
spill over
fence line

yet to fully
ripen
"ilka blade 'o grass has its ain drap 'o dew"

match the
morning quiet
tender thoughts… wistful feeling
imagine
two cups of coffee
not just one
yours table top
next to mine
me
next to
you

There

is still a lot
pass time
now dated
time
of
alternate reality
either w/words or with
lovers
roundabout way of memory wall
lurking today in my brain pan
Nancy n I ate a hand full of shrooms
were linked in right brain left brain
fribro cellular chemical psychedelic aware + oblivious
yet... we both sat on a San Francisco hillside
positive if we tried to walk
we would fly off an be swallowed bay water
dunked... laughing... gazing at each other
kaleidoscope bug eyes... dreaming wide awake
as we
wandered to her house
at day's end... she stared at her wall
told
me she always knew she picked correct colors
painted... but was now sure of it
for that one afternoon
we were one person in two bodies
then came real life again
She went off to China... I fell into a cocaine ditch
fell deeper... to points of near terminal velocity

on her return… ultimate sadness
"what have you done?" there were no
words to answer
she left… went to Bali
never came back or sent a post card
life… now… is looking back
on 38 years ago
with not a shred of guilt sand storm dust bunny bad mojo
or
who I was I am not now
every few years
I look at her picture… there is no reason to cry
that one afternoon
we were one person
in two bodies… if ya get that gold ring once
rejoice be glad in it
now
alone… surrounded with books
shadow bones bits of paper poems
argue w/my own what if's or what ever's
in… time took time… on Thursday
I will be 70 sober a long long time
yet… that afternoon lingers like
any sweet reflection should

A Bill Murray

weekend
as in Caddie Shack
but not
a gopher
no
fire ants
wack a mole... dig a hole
blending up potions
devoid of emotions
as in "strapped" bandana... floppy hat
boots... n gasoline... ASCEND... industrial strength
oil base toxic trauma supplied by quartermaster core
all because that one potted tree
was a hideout... secret headquarters... massive
bunker fortress of
perfectly aligned geometric maze of
chambers... escape routes... highway long
paths to forage... collect... bring back tribute
to engorged queen... layers of white pupa millions more
of these little bastards
wouldn't ya just know it
two days of combat
deck side this morning
I mourn em... they never had a chance
ecology nature balance harmony
not here baby... they never had a chance
a Dante like circle of this piss ant hell
is now... I think I killed that tree too
but... my yard is safe again
from welts... agony of itch... bitch bit for a final time

The Wicked Queen

who never
says
what she means

only what worded
proclaim intended to
make one
believe her benevolence
is real

only later to gather
with other witches… cackle
pretending to be
a
will 'o wisp

who's claws n acid heart
are
always hidden

Naughty

girl
skirt a swirl
fear to fall
fear to fly
a bit
too easy to make cry
looking back
it was a pleasure
to meet you

The Way

some bugs n snakes
use bright colors to
warn they are *toxic*
I wish what's her name
would
have
worn glow in the dark
underwear

Afternoon Rain

cloud cover lingering
cooling down
enough to
sit outside
G. Green, + B B Fall
sidewalk cafe in Saigon
speaking hushed
over… what next tragic adventure
would arrive to a behind
broken glass top… stone walls
that have watched for 1600 years
one war or another
with stoic silence
Gram says to Bernard
"lives to be lost money to be made"
sips his Pernod… n… Mr Fall answers
yes
but
"the women are so beautiful"

World's Oldest Woman

says the secret
is to
stay kinda drunk alla time

ha
well
I get
that n
ya don't gotta be drunk
on hooch
ya
can
be drunk
on smooch

I am
I gonna live
to a million
if half drunk counts
loopy zilly dilly me

I match her
three beers n shot
to my
five a day love poems
day dreams
plots n schemes
to see
her

and she knows damn well
who I mean

Space Rocks

ozone layer
pimp + player
rain forest sprinkler system
drought... fire... tropical storms
mass shootings
a host of body sick... food... air... bad water
O amma o abba... all the ships at sea
o dear me
if you spend an hour
n scour
news blues true or made up bullshit
ya go starkers
bonkers... cronkers... hide under the bed
hold yr aching head
scared some unseen force
gonna strike ya dead
crapola... shineola sterno mayonnaise
oil+water
dip stick... head gasket... cracked blocks
leaking valves... timing chain sprockets
nub worn... smoke n mirrors
all of it... not fit to print
then she walks by... you know her
that one who has that twinkle
sashays hey big boy ya wanna play
on that note... newspaper trash can liner
will she be minor... slip slide sideways
down carpet stairs... abandon all cares
the rest

you could get hit by a bus
so why fuss

Over the Moon

there was a time
I promise you
when my birthday
was not "exactly"
a cause to celebrate
as in "dat mother fucker ain't dead yet"
or... my own... path of stumble bum bullshit
now
overwhelmed with fond and sweet
wishes... took me a few years now
more en I care to mention
gettin my act in order
watching my wake... keeping my side of the street
clean
as this minute there are a few fishing reels a-soak
to be reassembled as I come n go
keyboard to work bench
glad for one more day... never mind years
years count
days count more... each one a gift
day light wrapping paper
lies cross a rain wet road
to
bottle up... bits of last night's star shine
leave off
old man... get busy stay busy
a top of the morning to you all
"n the rest o the day too"

1966

Mary Anne
first girl I kissed
back from Vietnam
on Taylor street… and Pacific
green eyes long hair
looking at me
with sadness
calling out to my aura
"where have you been what have you done?"
inside color is so clear
shrouded by a dark mist of
pain blood tears… a fear that she
said scared her… then she kissed
me before I could kiss her
we spoke of the future… she said to me
I recall tone intent vibrations of words
"you will need a lot of time. more time than I
am willing to spend, but only love can let those colors
come out"
I never saw her again

52 Years Ago

ok I was 18 in Vietnam
let me see if I can just run
this waka noddle down
in '56 a bit longer en that ago
under duress... from Dulles
Ike sent Iron Mike n 600 troopers to
that swamp... for to defend economic policy
nothing more nothing less
as a "workers paradise" drank em self dead
Never forget 911 (I know I jump around)
Nixon killed 30,000 people a week
in Cambodia... (who cares?) right
be glad for Gerry Ford... he only hurt ya
with golf balls
then comes Ronny Ray gun
at about nine times a number a week
as died in twin towers
all over Central America (who cares?)
great googa mooga Clinton Bush both
as even Obama now
plays two tunes on one piano
and again an economic policy
divide that to this day...
has us all either in credit card debt
student loan hell or like me
just ditter pitter stumble fritter
what the fuck over... over and over
to today
let us remember JFK

as all ya really need to know
is from Dylan… n leaders n parking meters
or
"don't let the sound of your own daemons drive ya crazy"
better living thru chemistry
pills pot hooch n acid
all fall down
no news is good news
ya gotta
be ready to do more with less
they confess
in the show room
selling some hedge fund guy
a new Ferrari… yup
you change your oil regular hear me
an old Ford Falcon drives by
with
better days written in blood on the side

TED Talk

I have no
idea
who Sara Jones is
but she took me
sideways outta no place
with one remark
"your offense is more about you than me"
as if
culture. race. gender. money lack of too much of
or only
thin lip bigots
who live in fear
then… from another no place
"if I am happy you can not offend me"
OK… nuff said

CIB

proudly am one
proudly wear one
coney island boy
combat infantry badge
with
this now "trending" art retrospective
about that slice o Brooklyn
I muse
about what was
bungalow heaven
became project building hell
over
a space from 10 to 16 years old
I use to pick blueberries… catch pogies
(sun tan lotion on a French Woman at bay 19)
meeting two twin sisters from California… sweet day that
was
now… Weegee photos… kum quat squat say it ain't so Joe.
n lots of "nostalgia" that combat badge
well
I got a good book outta that
now
MIDWAY MOVES BOARDWALK DREAMS
soon my
dear readers soon

Reach Back

OK 1967 living
in a lower east side
railroad flat 299 E 2nd st
with Patty Keen
who would later have
my daughter Mary… a couple years later
her sister was not
exactly my go to in-law
by a long shot… any way
Patty invited Sara over
for dinner right?
"can i bring my new fella"
sure… no problem
I am resigned to
it… but not really feeling all that
excited? cheerful? happy?
I only mention this today as
it is Mary's birthday
I am pretty sure she knows the story
anyway
all bang bang on metal door
opens to a bathtub kitchen
and and and
this new Fella? o me you can
not make up life movie looks
it is my younger brother Tommy, who I have
not seen since I got back from Vietnam
we both instant iggy up screw down any
sign of prior knowledge or relation

o such a nice time
over pork chops n veggies with
for us a really good bottle o wine
as we sit and fire up
a bit o da columbian
Sara is being really nice to me
we spill da beans
ya couldda heard a gnat fart
they sister-stare at each other
Tommy goes into his carny barker jive
I am
like o well double yr pleasure double yr fun
chewin on my pipe like doublemint gum
all four of us later moved to 533 E 5th
two floors from each other
months of family sort of frolic
Happy many more years my
bright eyed so sweet loving baby girl

Can Not Help Myself

Only one day a year
nope
Emerson said be thankful
for everything, good and bad
it all leads to development
well
I gotta say
there are sure a few moves
I wish had not made
not location, desperation
filling a no where place
in outer space, only
to hide my face
from display
Now
the supposed leaders of power (me I'm powerless)
act like third grade idiots
my weenie is bigger than your weenie
my bombs are bigger than your bombs
holy hoppin hamarabies
jumble mumble shake and bake the flesh off the bones
the battlefield full of painful moans
Just for today
(one day at a time, what a concept)
look someone you love
dead center
tell them you love them, show it, be it, then let it spread
like bees make honey
birds make music

dogs howl cats meow snakes slither, branches wither
all around up and down in and out some have
some are without
us, all of us, some of us, none of us
no matter
one face at a time lifted, smiles
says so sofly. I love you
more, I don't think so

Banjaxed

that an
you lot couldn't
organize a piss up in a brewery
I am now
calling HER… n she knows who
my muse
my amuse
my word sling badda bing
gobsmack te ra nog… cara
of now
till then
an
maybe when
we are ghosts together
n
scare da willy outta billy
n
all the snicker bicker bunch
who annoy HER

Lexonography

exfoliate elaborate extemporize
personify articulate
yea buddy you do that
like bo jangles dances
me
I make it up
outta torn tshirts...... soiled blue jeans
n pot of coffee beans
but
in consort... resort... slang bang be bop
tip top... fulla throw it
all
in da pot
what says hot
is cooked to not a lot
but
feed yr head... spend time in bed
have all the bluster buster M5 motorway
shoes
news... bit of peruse... giggle n snarl
"you old dog" ya said
well... not being able to hear birds sing
was a tragic bit of last week
today... I see ya... I hear ya... n only can go
say bad waddya hear waddya know

Love

well one guy
I talk to a lot
Roberto Silva
another Kevin Duncan not as often
love them both
I really do
most my ole pals
are gone now
Brazil... doy doy... taught me how
to get "over" my self
Plunking Duncan taught me
how to "read" war n tie good knots
as I get older... I find the best of life's lessons
are learned w/ that acceptance
only love brings... even if
so far away as they both are
I know they know

Lozzem Game

carny talk
for shut it down
I awoke from
a strange dream
big garage door... w/ a storm door inside
where it would do
no good
but
it opened too high... could not find
a hook or long enough pole
to close it
so found a ladder
as I climbed up
music started to play
a funeral dirge... in some language never heard
before
w/ a new ear infection... my voice echo inside
like talking into a tin can
meaning?... o dear
"often broken sleep leads to creative thinking"
stumped
garage doors squealing open are a sound
in my cells
like temple bells... fog horns... soft whispers
from lovers
as days go by

Disturbed

and in this
dream
I am yelling
at someone
"who is your therapist?"
there is a an
old fashioned bus fare box
n
one of those change dispensers
worn on a belt
but who
I was asking and why
are not revealed
bus engine is silent

Somewhere

even in
most tender of hearts
is
a hard spot
bitter part... so like a simple cell oyster
let that
sand pebble
heal over
to
become a pearl
of love
a windless morning prayer
from me
to you

A Bit

frightening en lighting moody melodramatic
like a movie
not a dream
some many room apt... in
a city I have never been in
with a few repairs needed
(I know the cars came from Velvet fan page)
a Simca and a big round Buick both
red n white
a woman with lots of clothes
on... like a layered look... but in n out of focus
no idea how I got there who she was
why I was dreaming it... as I was dreaming it
I kept trying to figure out the triggers
reference points... but none of the objects
or furniture as familiar as it seemed
had ever been part of my life... even recall some
wonderful old wood kitchen pieces in frisco
no
this was strange again scary but I was
not
scared
a few times we looked at each other
as she asked me to fix this or that
adjust the window... tighten up a vent
get the car started pull this extra
stuff to the curb... one woven char was a lion
one was this I am sure some design fawn over
dead in New York upper east side kind of

period thing or another
anyway
she makes some tea n crumpets
(I know laugh me n tea n crumpets)
any way I see this Icon on the wall
and all of a sudden dream fold open to
like some Elvira Maddigan or some other
sappy love movie
an I really see her face
"can it be you?" isay "tis me" has been
since I was sold… and abused
after you left me 49 years ago
no no no
(not a bit of this ever happened in my life
but in this drama dream scape it was real as death or taxes)
"we were to be married… you went off to war…
it was cruel for a year but some man bought me
and left me all this pile of dead memory walls"
she knew some people I know n I knew some
ones she did… then it turns sort of Fellini n we
go to this woman priest who is a carnival barker
n high roller of tarot card n lace face place of
spend money get predicted or really get evicted
who knows
I woke up… lie there… what the fuck was that
a complication explanation reflecting on
I went to war a fresh face fat boy… who loved poems
n the idea of love
came back a thousand yard stare
this
dream
was why when who what was
some kind of dump out a give a fuck not basket
n move on
waking up at 2:53 on facebook
proves it was frightening and enlightening

Ms Albright n Ms Feminismo

say
all you girls are goin
to hell
if ya don't vote for
Hillary
as if
her bit of
sell out to all da neo con boys
is not
gonna bring hell to ya
when she is war queen
on
eggs n ham
o yes I am
she says

My Daughter

just tole
me
to get out
talk to people
fr real
not
bang this drum
a rum a pum pum
all day
all night
in the dark
who cares
the river is black
with toxic waste
Hillary in your face
if either she or an elephant
get elected
you can be
sure
of tpp… n worse
OK Mary I hear ya
outta here
am i

At Dinner

a six minute dissertation
from a five year old
on "night mare moon assorted little pony some are
good some you have to be careful cause they might
not be really nice even if they tell ya they are nice
n I know this cause some kids are like that too"
OK
so
I put down my fork
look over
n try really hard not
to stare
even if my yap is hang open
never... and add to
pause arm wave
serious
to
giddy
back to serious again
then
all I could
do
is bust out some pistachio gelato
take a look at
my granddaughter
and be
spell bound... bust button
proud
n glad to
be alive

A Good Guy With a Gun

not
funny
not
fun
most
if not
all
these paper target
commandos
would
run
a group
of real combat vets
just made
hash
of
this dash to
arm baboons cartoons over weight myopic morons
as some
version of an "unregulated militia"
who
when first shots get
fired
shit splatter those
fancy
toy soldier outfits

Impossible

to either know
how or why
a mention of location
can trigger "events… time… places gone"
Philadelphia… I bet I have not thought
of that city since Rocky came out
but
spring semester at Philly College of Art '67
I was an artist model and worked nights
at the ZU ZU room as a bouncer
My Brother made book bar side… ,at
The Parker Hotel
I was in love with a really wild gal
(whose father had been blackballed by McCarthy)
any way she ran off
with my motorcycle an another guy
to Mexico… and I went n stole another bike
n went back to New York
where I met my Daughter's Mother
whose father was also given
the McCarthy "are you now or have you ever been
a member of the communist party?"
he was… and had to play piano in the Symphony
till he could teach again… many years later
any way
how location… or mention of
can find a mural painted on brain cells
out of "the still dark past"
is why I am

so glad
I have lived long enough
to have
lived
enough
to write it down now

Harmony

not sold
at your
local commercial outlet big box or order online
nope
ya might have to
had acquired some
yak n paddle
decent shoes
maybe good binoculars
but
what produces
natural aware
alive... in consort... attending to
being part of
meditation... explanation... memory or free thought
is
quiet
beyond any recorded posted distractions
alone
on some back fork
only birds n whispering leaves
yea harmony peace
tranquil breathing
the rest
is
all a steady trod... plod
to
an evermore dirt nap

Made It

not one
mention
of
anything
I can not
hold... see... smell... taste or hear
nope
now
I got get my beddy-by
fore
I
fuck that up

Forgiveness Sunday

start of Great Lent
if I have
in word or in any way
offended any one
here
forgive me... as I forgive any
and all
I am no longer Relgious
however
I find comfort in rituals lives of Saints
parts of a few different belief systems
Canons... (tomorrow the one of St Andrew of Crete)
fasting... and being repentant
over loud or vulgar or clumsy
lust full or not accepting others rights
I seek to be
in harmony with cosmic mystery
not
angry sad lonely tired or despondent
as I go sleep
less I sleep unto death n be caught by the wolf of souls
n
your own system of renew contemplate or be
as baffled as I am
at all news blues information at a mouse click
with more questions than answers

Peck Slip

coal chute
pier 9
alley ways
hand trucks
I am 15
hauling boxes
all over
Fulton Fish Market
making thirty fifty bucks a day
pilfer some fresh fish deelish
n bring em home
scallops… shrimp… a few filet
n Pop cook em up
life has turns… n bridges… true
but
when it was simple it was
easy… then… and easy now
fresh fish deelish

My Father

never had a company
or an Enterprise
for me to
inherit... no wage slave... day by
week paycheck
survival
truthfully I was
ashamed of his
honesty... acceptance
was way more attracted to
wise guys... steal it... fuck it...
what they gonna do
put ya in da Army n send ya to Vietnam
bet yr ass they would
then some years of rebellion
anger... not caring sharing not giving a fuck
women... love... my daughter... were
like... these barriers to either succumb to
or avoid
now... yup this minute... after doing that
same paycheck dance... (even if there were some lost years)
I recollect a passing sentence
"ya get what ya need if ya don't moan bout what ya want"
Rest Patsy... my Dad... my Pop... I am ashamed
of being ashamed of you
when now I struggle every day
to be half as honest as you

To Mourn

in silence
only to
remember
a line from
a great poet
Li-Young Li

"all ticketed passengers
please proceed
to the gate
marked
Evening"
I could
never say it better

Mistaken Identity

after years
of looking
only to discover
looking was not the answer
a better question was
why do I look
"as if love was a salve to heal my empty heart"
not... person place or thing
no external support... affection... sex drugs or rock n roll
can soften calcified marks in
an aura... marked dark early
by rejection... shame or disaffection
took a long time... to change colors
from dark to a pale yellow... like a daffodil
that was shades of magenta n lonely place
I can still see her face... now 50 years later
"only love will heal you... it will take more time
than I am willing to spend"
repeat... over n over
til... "she came she saw she left"

Down Shift

as turn 2
comes up
n she is drift a bit
ease up on
acceleration
gently
turn her
straight
again
an look not back
but down
as her second shift point
is
engaged
she breathes a bit steady now
but wants
a finish line
flag
so
sweet baby
tag it don't lag it
n
keep yr finger on the gas

Two

my favorite guys
Ole Hardcore n Jack Large
both come
out today
n
said
enough of political
fol de roll... fub da dub
rub da tub... mug be smug
my guy yr guy
that guy this guy
ass bust never trust
any of em
so
given that FOREVER CHARLOTTE
was da cover of T
mag
n had a picture of her
from 73... no more tell me
I hear em
fuck this noisy
bunch of
braggarts boasters coasters slip shod
shimmy shammy whimmy whammy
pile of poo
hey
me n you
an Charlotte too
Novena... Vespers... Matins... Comp line

Midnight office… prayers n love poems
as if now
some way somehow…

This poet goona do what
that poet does
ole Double down Danska Doubinski does
too

We Were

middle of

speak... phone line
jabber... I do go on
over heard
over cast
blue moon night

choir sound
frog croak
as if
every body
don't know
froggy be a courtin

gribbit gribbit
I managed to get
in a few
be still my heart
lines my self

as her throaty laugh
n
whisper giggle
made
me
blush

A Time

when I was
alone scared in
some jungle pass
on some unnamed mountain
in Asia
n only humming a Joan Baez
song
kept me sane
may
she
always
be
forever young

Eye Blink

take not
today
or
five minutes from now
for granted
sun light shifts
window blind lifts
pale riders who are
not Saints
but... demons... intent
on
our destruction
in eleven days
or
ninety months
behind bars
or
free as any
passing stage coach
human... animals
having some
positive impact
can
reverse or move
hour glass... time face... motion or
in place
rest now
take no chances
other

than
taking all chances
love
dust
dirt... bread... water... air
care
do not
despair

Late

for me
trash out hash out lines
lines
one complete sentence
is a major feat
for me

She had this ring to her laughter
that made talking to her a feat of happy feet
a symphony to the ear.
I can
do it, if I try
however
I love just
stacking words
fly by
skip from
here to next month
back to
years ago
young time
chasing all
noisy numbers
rubber tumblers
water water all
around
late at night not a sound
only
memory smile that one above
line
to her voice

Fly Boy

fly boy
green smoke my mark
forward paddy dyke tree line over
green green bean have visual over
fly boy fly boy tango foxtrot romeo over
green bean green bean dig deep for light up over
slow mover banks guns ablaze
trees fall like matches… smoke fire noise
fly boy fly boy oscar tango over
the poetry
of war

Possible

between laundry
road signs
that
could say
something different
today
or a turn
not taken
cheerful
or faking
risks not taking
clouds a shaking
talk to me
point out directions
with
some old ideas
days gone
stacked
like cord wood... piles
of maybe
found or forgotten
along whatever street light
attraction was
ignored

Love Affairs

can be like
hurricanes
building off shore
gaining strength
velocity intensity
or
dissipate lose ferocity
over mundane regular bits
day to day
past memories
future dreams
best ones
both weather love connections
pass over but
remain
named
called on
both history and present
no body knows
that
is mystery of
storms, boys girls you me her him them
palm trees
waterfalls… kisses
glasses of tea

I Am

re-living
my childhood
n facebook
is my Saturday morning cartoons
all Winky Dink magic screen
crayons on make
a zinger or two
only thing different only thing new
that
horrible sugar pops... n sour milk
is
gone
now
I salute all
my pose post picture meme gang
of
peanut gallery attendees in
consort n contrast
bombast... chuckle snort... n
Princess summer fall winter spring
is
now a 100 years old
in a tepee dream
I had
64 years ago

Sometimes

no alla time
if ya
don't know what to
do
don't do nothing

say not ask not be not
a royal ass bite
meaning well
or saying maybe
this
maybe that
balls it up
like back lash bait casters
birds nest twigs grass hay assorted bits
of nonsense

love affairs only work
when both of ya
want em to
not
when one of ya
needs em to

nothing on life's chart plot page
is
worse than
dead zone areas
not navigable air land or sea

some things are best
when somethings
are not

5:10 a.m.

woke up grumpy n sad
of places I been
people I knew... and know
hungry bears
die off bees
birds n other creatures losing places
safety... absolute fuckwad dipshit morons
running for office
excess consumption... material greed
never even mind paper stack assholes who
breed on other people's "investments"
sick to my soul
every artist... no matter who
use what is already here
wanna make statues go da junkyard
use ole bumpers n doors
wanna paint... mix your own
writers save paper... be aware of waste
this is indeed our only place
straight up... sustain
not complain
we are in a process
of destroying our rock in space
smug face
callin em self "rich"
so... I must... for a few days
sort of pull in my own horns
bassoons... baboons... chitter chatter snarl
moan... decry... I am scared

not afraid to admit it
between hate n fear n profit
I sit here
amazed
peace on earth good will towards men
is
a puddle soaked Christmas card
been marked "return to sender"
no such address no such zone

Easy To

once upon a time
till
yr ass falls off
debate... reiterate... delegate
manners... fence side
chats
back room spats
telling this guy
that guy is telling lies
while refuse to look
in yr eyes
cause his take is just as
shady
man love a lady
in passing
I had someone tell me
about "hope in heaven"
or milk n honey other side
blind broke deaf dumb
n furthermore
who tole ya
Adam and Eve
were solo units n maybe
there is
some mystery
when someone
asks me "what do you believe?"
I tell em straight up
depends on
my mood...

Clutter

litter
Japanese woman
tells ya… it must bring joy
or
toss it
well
my hoarder problem is not
material
no
spiritual
emotional
exclusion delusion
confusion
if
anybody… had to think like me
just for an hour
park that dump truck over here
pull that madness
ear to ear
bust a move o dear
piddle paddle fiddle faddle
where did I put my
keys

Long Ago

My dear dead brother
was
born with a speech impediment
he was smart but
unable to voice it
how ever
give some heat score or jack pot
Our Mother mad as a hornet
"you wait 'til your Father gets home"
he worked nights
Tommy would run down
jetty side n trot line some live eels
n
put em in da sink... Pop come home
n see em
long as we had not burned da house down
dem eels made him so happy
course she would come in
already two beers down
n start raggin him bout us
n He would be singing some off key show tune
n fry up dem eels
n tell her
"boys will be boys"
I am tearful at this memory
rest dear Tommy... rest now since
you are back home

Domestic Advice

remember helpful hints
from Heloise?
well
if you put yr
coffee beans in
da grinder
in da dark
very good chance
yr coffee will
make you
bark

No Bake Cookies

shadow pan
flat
sugar free... ginger snaps

as days pass
seven grain homemade bread
sweet mangoes... plums... pears
dragon fruit n avocados
big as melons

walks beach side
steady
ready

in love all over
again
felt table poker games
fly tie bench
fingers bent... eye repair soon

dancing with
my darling
at the falling of the moon

that mending fences... keeping my
nasty ass clean
my foul some time yap
shut

all is well in Swamplandia
midnight office

blessed be the name
of God, blessed be
all my friends
you
we
us
all of them

now an 'til death do us part
not a marriage but
an
arrangement… that means the same

Silent Sorrows

door way suffused light
leading
up a flight
of carpet stairs
a face chase
place
she looked out
an upstairs
window saw
him drive by
waved a ring less fingered hand
objects in mirror are closer than they appear
echo bounce sad love song
sung
in discord harmony
off key
each note choke
breathing thru tears
oblivion hi way
always
yesterday

Dust

ash
bones skulls
remain
we
have been
here
we left
among those
gone
love songs
play
invisible stereo
of
our hearts
no
matter what time
of
day
it is

Jan '64

particular bad patrol
tight ass fire fight
bugs... really bad bugs
bit to shit
Maddy is welts n itchy
on commo... out of his ear
I call
back base camp
ice up some San Miguel Dark
n
get me a Thracian swab
two cans of Dole Pineapple juice
n
I don't care how
but some flowers
so
drag ass I mean slug ass
back
Mad Dog is patrol leader so
he gotta check in
head count n supervise
stack arms n visual
all cowboys check in
I run
hooch side
Honley (God rest him)
had all I asked for

My main Man Mr Terrific
just about

done
really… drops his gear
I call out… come to poppa big boy
he
sees a bucket with ice n beer
these scraggle ass weeds
n a big can of Dole
HAPPY NEW YEAR MOTHER FUCKER
I tell him
he busts out
shouts out
you meddle dick sad excuse for a paratrooper
I love you too much

war… frolic n fun
o yea… the bug juice balm
really was a big deal
some guys get it really bad
me I eat way too much garlic
they hate me

Plants... Planets... People

twas fifty years ago
today
I come back from Asia
relieved to be alive
troubled to be so
also
now
looking back
I have no idea if anyone
can "really understand" coming outta 18 months
of combat
to San Francisco... in 1966
to
say... smoking plants... hearing
about planetary alignments... moons
n people who could "see" auras
yup
today
I am amused
sad
a bit of both
so
fifty more years
I
doubt it

Was More Than 40

plus years ago
best deal I ever
made
trade Dr Moss…
for a clutch job on his Jaguar XKE
to deliver a baby
my baby Marme Coco Bearme
all her life
I told her
never felt bout any one
like I feel bout
you
then… a bit after she
had her baby
Lillian Bunny Hop a long sweetness
she called me
"I get it now Dad… I do"
another calendar page
wisp roll over
days go by
I still don't feel bout any
one
like I do my daughter
but
her daughter is pullin up close
in turn 6 on this race way
we call life
quick cue Joan.,… n may you
always be… "forever young"
L

Living History

pages pages all fall down
static electric movements
howling back reaching forward
why I
wrote THEN N NOW
today
a photo... some 40 years old
or so
captures encapsulate time events days
laughter n pain
all assembled like a Greek chorus
wags nags busted knuckles bloody noses
we all had lot o hair
girlfriends... sidekicks home boys
dealers squealers stand up lie down
alley way exchanges of
so much money it is funny
now
sitting trying to make
a check book not bounce like
we bounced bopped hopped
n gave not a fuck
bout tomorrow
joy n sorrow... bindles full of
marching powder... smokin Js foggy haze
of
yes static electric play grounds... grind beans tight jeans
fast bikes... soft leather seats
swearing we could not be beat

old now... living history on
books of faces
remembering those places
ashes ashes all fall down... narco bunko jail cells
self abusing hells... bells... paint it write it
call it what you will
life fill... sitting here
now
magazine subscription or water bill

Musta Been

8 or 9 years old
Mrs Caspadora
who lived a
few houses away
sweet rolls... n muffins
raking her leaves... shovel her walk
she would give me
treats an some quarters
one time
with just two dimes
at dish pitch
I won this carnival glass green bowl
I gave it to her
she put it round hallway table
with a doily
under it
n pinched my
cheek
bella bambini... domenico
I have no idea why
I remember this now
love I guess

Given a Gift

then
only learning
how to use
it
now
somehow
she walks in rain
mentions pain
of
window reflected
what
could have been
neon noise

Azzuro Bene

a taste of
salt air grown
blueberries bungalow yard back
on 33rd St in Coney Island, where
Mr Caspadora had an arbor a bunch
of bushes concord grapes wild berries
all in the middle of some fantasy idea
of amusement park board walk beach
crowds from all over
(locals avoided the scene like the plague)
other than the carney razzes pin joint flim flam crew

Any way Mr Moses Mr Wagner Mr Beam
had this urban renewal plan
(stack em in brick sardine cans, fuck em they don't vote)
as the bulldozer the cement trucks the line of
cranes bully boy out of town contractors
came en mass this twelve year ole
(me)
wept in the scratchy crab grass vacant
of the grapes the bungalow the many year berry bush
I have had blueberries since
they never taste like those from when
Life was not a for sale operation
Mercy on the soul of that small Italian man
who made the best of what he had
sandy soil bayside breeze land

Go Away

you
soundless dream
of walls… painted streak
haunted faces
never
even saying
how are you?
only
staring
hollow eyed at
some place
distant

Sleepwalk

o dear me o my
a Dick Clark show
tape is floating round the page
Santo + Johnny... o man

I have on occasion been called "sappy"
well
tell ya what it was 1959
Dave Baby Cortez Roy Orbison...

on the radio mixed in was
heart tug steel pedal throb string
sleep walk
I danced slow for the first time
I remember her name face and
perfume... in a second floor flat
on Coney Island

seeing it today
many years later... yesterday
came back... I was awkward, unsure scared silly
of gettin a chubby

she I swear I can hear it pitch tone perfect
"don't dance, float... I will show you"

that and Anny had a baby
uhuu uhuu
kept me alive
in Vietnam

I met her again we were both in
our twenties… she remembered tole
me "you were so sweet"

SLEEPWALK BACK TO BROOKLYN
50+timeless years ago

Ode to Dancing

well I told my pal
Ian
bout my cousin Bernadette
teach me how to dance
way back... when
I was in love with Pamela Pierce
n... {she told} me... if ya step on her feet like ya do
mine... she will never kiss ya
o boy... do I remember that... Johnny Mathis
n 'til 12th of never
n now... I have not "danced" in a lot of years
however
I made a bad bare foot mistake
on my drive way... at 93 n blaze glaze sun hot
asphalt... dance?
well... if oooch oooch... ouch ouch...
in knees to elbow not touch down
I be one
dancing clown

Radio Love Song

recall
me
dancing
somewhere
between A Summer Place
n
Run Around Sue

Like the TV Show?

Ya want yr life to be like the TV show where the guy gets the girl or the crime is solved between commercials... or indeed do ya want that dark or light mystery... who is that masked man... was she really smiling at you... did that glance mean more than a chance... are the window lookers who thank the Sun... n love the moon... earth spin... the sound of a rattle wrench loose up wheel lugs... pale mist fog on the river top... a broken heart... that only really means ya had a heart to be broken... do you really want to know?... not me... explain the secret to cooking well... n keep the rest this wonder full dark or light mystery... time... or dreams of clocks... the wait for what is next... turn the next corner with a smile on your kisser... n ya might get a kiss back... scowl... n grump... n fuss... ya might as well take the buss

Air Water Salami Sandwich

and you
basic life needs
dishes, washed. floors clean
bed made
teeth brush toilet flush
all
over everyplace

wash face… kneel bedside
ask for
safety… health

a kiss
in thinking passing
caress embrace
smile face to face

all before good night
my love
that kiss was
for you

Restore

wings unto a
dove
sing you
quiet songs of
love
begone madness
infections
deflections
whisper
to her
that quiet
song of love

Simplicity

of shallow
water
or reflections
on
ideas... art... moments of time
not
to over think
unravel or claim to
be
more aware
acceptance of
sand bottom geometric patterns
birds wings birds songs
poems
tomes
mystery novels
all
part
of
knowing
what ya don't know
is
restful knowing or saying
ya
do
is all
egocentric bullshit

Askance

daily
between
serious
delirious
pathos humor
figs dates
backward glances
impending romances
desultory predictions
shifting convictions
meet me half way
from coffee to
fresh spinach fresh caught fish
see a shooting star
make a wish
you know
we all do
daily dramas
impacted facts
torn from pages
of books
slow close your eyes
words dance
if all reading thinking
passing traffic unlock
secrets
back and forth
who am I
why am I here

or
way more important
why
is she
not here
speaking of
this endless mystery
called daily life

Wondering

words
said
in person
airy
conflict or equal
ones
read
alone

sorting trying to sort
meanings
never
printed in any dictionary
or translate to clarity

brain to heart
heart to brain
some come loaded
with romance
some
overloaded
with
pain

Brightly So

as paperwork
shopping
sort out
theater wear
for
down town neon

as only this
one
wish
will
you
be
mine

Tell Me

dear one
what
colors taste like
do
you feel the electric
in
my hand
holding yours
I do

each grain of
sand
microscopic bits of glass
bone shell time compressed
on
each beach

tell me
my love
as
sun set glow
do
you know
what
colors taste like

When

an entire list
of reasons
for this that
pitty pat... silly this silly that
no
longer can
be either used to
blame
explain
complain
facing 5AM
look around at internal
motivations... ruminations... memory bank
overdrawn
50 years ago next month
sittin on a Frisco hill side
kissing a girl with brown hair n green eyes
to
sittin on this porch
drinking coffee
declaring... demanding
what ever happened did
what might
as yet to
so

Umm Jumble Fly Getting By

are
we
what we read
eat
think
talk about
lay about
wishing upon a rock

take me
shake me
make
me
love you

no… in the last few days
I
have been from quiet
salon day what did they pay
spy books… tomes about saints
dead
so long now… only telling is
left… unless some relic
amber isotope contain

too much
information
my daughter tells me
"chill dude take a media break"

ok
then I call her
make up
poems I am scared to
write... cause I want them
so right
her hearing them
is best heard
alone
as we each change
voices to
suit our
moods

Midway Blues

snow blown wind
on the boardwalk
slate sky
window watchers wait for sun
the air itself is frozen

two old winos
huddle next to a barrel fire
smoking hand rolls
layers of clothes
plastic bag overshoes

jetty rocks tipped with ice
hard sand footsteps tide line
wash out sea foam
the air itself is frozen

Coney Island morning long
time ago

Me Too

a boy from Brooklyn
who left
5 decades ago
but
unlike poster boy
in Style section of da paper
today
I ain't got no
100 million dollar clout
ta bring back
shit
I bet I could not afford to
live under the boardwalk
where I used to run away from home to
n Pop would... just laugh
he be back
when he gets hungry enough
so true
a bit sad a bit blue
still fighting off a flu
n
wondering about you

Sisters

yes my family
in words
in space cyber
a few I even see
in person
Jen, Corina, I love you
Suzanne, Dana, Mona Lisa, Lisa, Antonia, Alicia,
Donna Lee, who I have known forever
some I just met
here or on the train
in the rain
over the terrain
of this kingdom by the sea
Judy and me
I am safe from
want
or need
It is the heart of you of me
you feed
I was so lost
afraid
not putting a single
word on the page
(not here because I was not here yet)
I lived on the river
spoke to fish and alligators
grunted to my coworkers
ignored most of the
rest

in toto
I was burned
before, war, crime, drugs, Dept of Corrections
twenty years of Teresa, my own Spirit guide
who always told me my danger was me
not anyone or anything else

Now after a bit of a spat
of chat
and shatter my soft dream
I can love you all not having
a secret or a scheme

Yes my sisters
lovers friends
who are allowing
me to be
what I was supposed to be
I found it in you

Mother's Day

Hard scrabble
daughter of the migrant
dust bowl bunch
who was
a plain spoken
steel willed woman

She had a son
she loved dearly
he was a part cowboy
part hell raiser
part lost boy (of the late '50s style)
with the leather jacket
duck tail hair cut
hot rod car and fight at the drop nickel

well there was trouble
small town bad blood
the judge gave him the coin toss
the Army or jail
it was common then

any way a year or so later
the fancy dress uniform
yellow envelope bearing
come a knocking
on the door

She was past grief
past loss
past despair

her husband (not the father)
came home found her
under the kitchen table
curled in a ball
cried out dried out beyond grief beyond despair

He was tender sweet
carried her up the stairs
she stayed in bed a couple days
told him to give the "blood money"
to the orphanage

The triangle folded flag
medal with the jump wings
combat infantry badge
stayed on the mantle
till one day she put it away

we went to see her
Maddy and I
she was back to growing food
raising chickens
keeping the house and yard
pin neat and clean

She did not have a lot
to say
as we wished her
a happy Mother's day
it was the saddest day
of my whole life

I Would Be Remiss

not to send a good
night kiss
twist
take sea
pics
for get to say
until that time
my dear
until that time
with
wave top
cross current
days
one glass of
ice tea
you
+
me

Yesterday's Ring

A love trophy
a medal of valor
for the vigil
now
as
Mother's day
approaches
when
have you (us, some of us, most of us all of us)
ever seen more
tender
patient
sunshine or sorrow
in Mom's eyes
sickness or health
better or worse
all
the vows
ever made
could not
even do the laundry
of Mama Bear, Mama Wolf,
tough tender hard soft patient or annoyed
it never matters
nobody ever did
or ever will
love you like
A Mother, can, does, will
now and forever

Collected

impacted
distracted confused
unsure but
willing
dare to dream
conditioned
miss mash of fun... cigars cars
women
songs
birds... sound of em both
voices
or echos of em
complications expressed
or denied
results factor
hollering matters
sitting alone
watching sound
hearing vision
as a few weeks ago
had
bitter bile compile
a mess of twisted truth
that
was
no truth at all
only more... my way or da hi way
bullshit... in bunches
o

today
be
book good to me
humility wins
all memory
is
as fleeting
as thoughts are

41716

let's go back
to when we needed each other
not used each other
for either profit or entertainment
this whole myth religion superstitious
cracks black cats Halloween... to
boy o boy my new iPone is keen

in the end
we die... transport? decompose? return to ash or bone
sightless n alone
to the very Mother of us all
this spinning rock
called home
does mom scold us
no
embraces us... as all loving mothers do
if
only we had been loving too
quick cue Louis... "an what a wonderful world"
o
dear me

Last Week

I got to see
some people who
have known me for
fifty years give or take
an
we all
were laughing
who would have
ever thought I would
wear an apron
and love house work
an act polite
one guy "substance"
he said
you have become a man of
substance
I did not
want any of
em to
see me cry

Connective

captivated
charmed
entwined
lips hips
hints of gardenia + jasmine
amber eyes
silk hair... smiles
side glances
then I woke up
shadow night light
no perfume... only
dried salt tears
on the pillow

A Love Poem

to a motorcycle
cause
I sure not having
much luck with women lately
any way
47 rigid frame 67 shovel head motor
Chocolate George n me
built it at Torelli Import Auto
on Fell St... San Francisco glory days
simple 4 over front end
dog bone risers with
a Tibet prayer bell hung between
forks... with old blue plate reflector button
plate surround says "safety first"
stock chain drive with over size rear wheel n tire
front wheel is diamond spoke n drum brake
Avon white walls front n back
painted Burgundy by Ernie Rat Wong
one off hippie hand stitch thunder bird seat
Laurel Ann pin stripe fenders in yin yang globe
final drive tweak with lake slide fuel injector
electrics all touched up... spark plug wires clear
stain less steel pipes... baffled but throaty
one other hippie leather attach
a saddle bag says "RETURN TO SENDER"
rode that chopper for years
long gone now... stolen while I was doing time

Was a Time

I could make
motors sing
baritone
n tires screech tenor
gears never slipped
u joints never broke
oil + water were good
now...
well we
all
get
old

She

speaks of night flowers
blooming from
commingled laughter
ha
soon
he like so many others
will be belladonna
nightshade
of
anger… spite. no one can ever
live up to her
daddy

Unable

to discern
if it is stuck
or a sticking point
trash talk
snipe wail to beat
castanets and trombones

watching this side
call that side
wrong… in equal measure
add to that
this extreme failing
of my own
to accept life on life's terms
dictate
masturbate in words
all over the page

empty house
a room I arranged with
about the most tender care
I have ever been able to
show feel or do
sits as empty
as the bones
in the grave
I dug back yard
to bury poems she sent me
as I am now

only a piss down the leg
bad memory

home again
unable to discern if
it is stuck
or I am
wallow swallow my
sadness anger grief
sticking point
as each day
I race home to
see
posts
I was never
meant to

Some Times...

the past
is like a stray dog
only wanting to
be safe
from Darkness

Other times...

presently that
dog
is well fed
n
asleep in the sun

Neural Pathways

my
first three ideas
are
mostly
immoral
illegal
or
fattening… default set
to idea 5 or 6
daily
a cluttered mind
hasty early routines
often lead to
abrupt directional changes
so
steady on boy
not necessarily straight
but
always forward.
damned cake for breakfast did
it
again

Holy Shitarolley

o I do so
wish
she were
here

dark as night at
5:23 wind rain
booooom lighting
tree bend palm fronds
dance separated exasperated
right on down the road

o I do so wish she were here
cuddle
bank
blanket tank
sheets shake
love make

wooooo tropic
storm afternoon

Two Rods

one spoon
one diving yo zuri lure
bridge lights
shadow lines
alone
at 4 a.m
casting
thinking
or not
drop retrieve… hypnotic repetitive
water top love
on a last day
of a first month
in
a new year

Been Shot

been locked up
crashed a bike
at 80... bike hurt worse en me

subjected myself
to about
9 forms of self-abuse
(not wanking cause that is fun)
no drugs crime... self-decay
mental torture of
sinus style chuck up
come to alley way
at 4 a.m.... alone so sad
there are no words for

just a half month ago
this woman tole
me
"hit the bricks... beat it... I am moving on with my life"

I take the bullet
road rash
even "incomprehensible demoralization"
just
for a phone call
it is not gonna happen
how
long will this
scar take to heal

love... idea of love... attractions stronger than steel

now
linger finger tap
like play the "O I done her wrong now she gone"
blues
on a computer

this modern
life is fucking a trip

Another Week

light change hour move
n
await my SS check
not a complaint
in any direction
old enough to know better
n
finally smart enough
to act like it
ahhh
Sunday evening
street light bounce
window frame
shadows on
my newly cleaned tile floor
why worry
what for

Looking Back

Metro motors
Columbus Ave SF
bout 68 or so
Uncle Geno… an old Hudson mechanic
put me to work
called me knuckle head
"fa Domenico basta nole loppa de testa"
(stop or I smack you in da head)
old 50s cars of people who
knew him for years
no estimate no chatter
drop off the car
come back pay
an bring some grappa or a calzone
n Geno
slap my hand
I try n grab a sip or a hunk
homemade cheese n ravioli
if only
I had not been
so ready to go mad
be bad
n have wild adventure
(still pissed off over Vietnam)
I would have got that shop
n been
a grumpy ole guy like he was
looking back… no telling

www.ingramcontent.com/pod-product-compliance
Lightning Source LLC
Chambersburg PA
CBHW022112090426
42743CB00008B/821